AF594391

RECIPE

Serves: Prep time:

Ingredients:

Method:

RECIPE

Serves: Prep time:

Ingredients:

Method:

RECIPE

Serves: Prep time:

Ingredients:

Method:

RECIPE

Serves: Prep time:

Ingredients:

Method:

RECIPE

Serves:

Prep time:

Ingredients:

Method:

RECIPE

Serves: Prep time:

Ingredients:

Method:

RECIPE

Serves: Prep time:

Ingredients:

Method:

RECIPE

Serves: Prep time:

Ingredients:

Method:

RECIPE

Serves: Prep time:

Ingredients:

Method:

RECIPE

Serves: Prep time:

Ingredients:

Method:

RECIPE

Serves: Prep time:

Ingredients:

Method:

RECIPE

Serves: Prep time:

Ingredients:

Method:

RECIPE

Serves: Prep time:

Ingredients:

Method:

RECIPE

Serves: Prep time:

Ingredients:

Method:

RECIPE

Serves: Prep time:

Ingredients:

Method:

RECIPE

Serves: Prep time:

Ingredients:

Method:

RECIPE

Serves: Prep time:

Ingredients:

Method:

RECIPE

Serves:

Prep time:

Ingredients:

Method:

RECIPE

Serves: Prep time:

Ingredients:

Method:

RECIPE

Serves: Prep time:

Ingredients:

Method:

RECIPE

Serves: Prep time:

Ingredients:

Method:

RECIPE

Serves:

Prep time:

Ingredients:

Method:

RECIPE

Serves: Prep time:

Ingredients:

Method:

RECIPE

Serves: Prep time:

Ingredients:

Method:

RECIPE

Serves: Prep time:

Ingredients:

Method:

RECIPE

Serves: Prep time:

Ingredients:

Method:

RECIPE

Serves: Prep time:

Ingredients:

Method:

RECIPE

Serves: Prep time:

Ingredients:

Method:

RECIPE

Serves: Prep time:

Ingredients:

Method:

RECIPE

Serves: Prep time:

Ingredients:

Method:

RECIPE

Serves: Prep time:

Ingredients:

Method:

RECIPE

Serves: Prep time:

Ingredients:

Method:

RECIPE

Serves: Prep time:

Ingredients:

Method:

RECIPE

Serves: Prep time:

Ingredients:

Method:

RECIPE

Serves: Prep time:

Ingredients:

Method:

RECIPE

Serves: Prep time:

Ingredients:

Method:

RECIPE

Serves: Prep time:

Ingredients:

Method:

RECIPE

Serves:

Prep time:

Ingredients:

Method:

RECIPE

Serves: Prep time:

Ingredients:

Method:

RECIPE

Serves: Prep time:

Ingredients:

Method:

RECIPE

Serves:

Prep time:

Ingredients:

Method:

RECIPE

Serves: Prep time:

Ingredients:

Method:

RECIPE

Serves: Prep time:

Ingredients:

Method:

RECIPE

Serves: Prep time:

Ingredients:

Method:

RECIPE

Serves: Prep time:

Ingredients:

Method:

RECIPE

Serves: Prep time:

Ingredients:

Method:

RECIPE

Serves: Prep time:

Ingredients:

Method:

RECIPE

Serves: Prep time:

Ingredients:

Method:

RECIPE

Serves: Prep time:

Ingredients:

Method:

RECIPE

Serves:

Prep time:

Ingredients:

Method:

RECIPE

Serves: Prep time:

Ingredients:

Method:

RECIPE

Serves: Prep time:

Ingredients:

Method:

RECIPE

Serves: Prep time:

Ingredients:

Method:

RECIPE

Serves: Prep time:

Ingredients:

Method:

RECIPE

Serves: Prep time:

Ingredients:

Method:

RECIPE

Serves: Prep time:

Ingredients:

Method:

RECIPE

Serves: Prep time:

Ingredients:

Method:

RECIPE

Serves: Prep time:

Ingredients:

Method:

RECIPE

Serves: Prep time:

Ingredients:

Method:

RECIPE

Serves: Prep time:

Ingredients:

Method:

RECIPE

Serves: Prep time:

Ingredients:

Method:

RECIPE

Serves: Prep time:

Ingredients:

Method:

RECIPE

Serves: Prep time:

Ingredients:

Method:

RECIPE

Serves:

Prep time:

Ingredients:

Method:

RECIPE

Serves: Prep time:

Ingredients:

Method:

RECIPE

Serves: Prep time:

Ingredients:

Method:

RECIPE

Serves: Prep time:

Ingredients:

Method:

RECIPE

Serves: Prep time:

Ingredients:

Method:

RECIPE

Serves: Prep time:

Ingredients:

Method:

RECIPE

Serves: Prep time:

Ingredients:

Method:

RECIPE

Serves: Prep time:

Ingredients:

Method:

RECIPE

Serves: Prep time:

Ingredients:

Method:

RECIPE

Serves: Prep time:

Ingredients:

Method:

RECIPE

Serves: Prep time:

Ingredients:

Method:

RECIPE

Serves: Prep time:

Ingredients:

Method:

RECIPE

Serves: Prep time:

Ingredients:

Method:

RECIPE

Serves: Prep time:

Ingredients:

Method:

RECIPE

Serves: Prep time:

Ingredients:

Method:

RECIPE

Serves: Prep time:

Ingredients:

Method:

RECIPE

Serves: Prep time:

Ingredients:

Method:

RECIPE

Serves:

Prep time:

Ingredients:

Method:

RECIPE

Serves: Prep time:

Ingredients:

Method:

RECIPE

Serves: Prep time:

Ingredients:

Method:

RECIPE

Serves: Prep time:

Ingredients:

Method:

RECIPE

Serves: Prep time:

Ingredients:

Method:

RECIPE

Serves: Prep time:

Ingredients:

Method:

RECIPE

Serves: Prep time:

Ingredients:

Method:

RECIPE

Serves: Prep time:

Ingredients:

Method:

RECIPE

Serves: Prep time:

Ingredients:

Method:

RECIPE

Serves: Prep time:

Ingredients:

Method:

First published in 2021 by New Holland Publishers
www.newhollandpublishers.com
ISBN: 9781760793371
10 9 8 7 6 5 4 3 2